EATS, TREATS & SWEETS

JOKES

LITTLE BOOK,
BIG LAUGHS

BY KIDS
FOR KIDS

Discover the
Oliver & Hope®
Storybook Series
at uhccf.org.

UnitedHealthcare
Children's Foundation®

ISBN: 978-0-692-60793-0

Manufactured in the United States of America.
First Printing.

Publisher: UHCCF/Adventure
Author: Meg Cadts and UHCCF
Contact: UnitedHealthcare
                 Children's Foundation

                 MN017-W400
                 P.O. Box 41
                 Minneapolis, MN 55440-0041

                 1-855-MY-UHCCF (1-855-698-4223)
                 uhccf.org

Find more laughs inside the **"Little Book - Big Laughs"** series at uhccf.org!

Now, this will make you smile.

Not only does this book deliver hours of good laughs, it also supports a good cause. All the jokes that appear in this book have been shared by the kids, and their families, many of whom have a direct connection to the UnitedHealthcare Children's Foundation (UHCCF).

UHCCF, above all else, is about delivering smiles to children and families that need it most. Since 1999, that mission has included awarding thousands of medical grants, totaling tens of millions of dollars. The sale of this book helps make those medical grants possible. So remember when you're smiling your way through the following pages, you'll be helping so many more smile along with you.

About UHCCF

UHCCF is a 501(c)(3) charitable organization that provides medical grants to help children gain access to health-related services not covered, or not fully covered, by their family's commercial health insurance plan. Families can receive up to $5,000 annually per child ($10,000 lifetime maximum per child), and do not need to have insurance through UnitedHealthcare to be eligible. UHCCF was founded in 1999. Since 2007, UHCCF has awarded more than 14,000 grants valued at over $36M to children and their families across the United States. UHCCF's funding is provided by contributions from individuals, corporations and UnitedHealth Group employees. To apply, donate or learn more, please visit uhccf.org.

PRESENTED TO YOU BY:

TO: _____

From: _____

My Favorite Jokes Are On Pages:

_____

_____

What do penguins eat for breakfast?

Ice Krispies.

Aditya P. | Cypress, CA

What are twins' favorite fruit?

Pears!

Allen L. | Boynton Beach, FL

Why was the salad cold?

Because she was lightly dressed.

Blaine P. | Alexandria, VA

What is the difference between a piano and a fish?

You can tune a piano but you cannot tuna fish!

Cameryn Q. | Monticello, MN

What do you call a cow that can't moo?

A Milk Dud.

Evie H. | Fishers, IN

What cookie can make you rich?

A fortune cookie!

Nicklaus H. | Wayzata, MN

What do you call potatoes sat on by an elephant?

Mashed potatoes!

Kylie F. | Ebensburg, PA

What's a duck's favorite vegetable?

Aspara-goose!

Nolan N. | Woodland Hills, CA

Did you hear the joke about peanut butter?

I'm not telling, you might spread it!

Baille M. | Floral City, FL

What is a cat's favorite dessert?

Mice-cream!

Mia C. | West Des Moines, IA

UnitedHealthcare Children's Foundation

Why did the Oreo go to the dentist?

Because he lost his filling.

Khloe A. | Frederick, MD

Who runs the candy farm?

The Jolly Rancher.

Brooke S. | Las Vegas, NV

What did the mommy tomato tell the kid tomato when he was falling behind in school?

"Ketchup."

Olivia E. | Willard, MO

What does the pig use to wash his hands?

"Ham" sanitizer.

Madison L. | Carlsbad, CA

What do you call a sheep covered in chocolate?

A chocolate bahhhhh!

Sofia N. | Hudson, FL

A man walks up to a hostess and says, "I hear you have the world record for being the fastest restaurant in the world."

The hostess responds, "Yes, we do. Here is your receipt. Thanks for coming."

Amber J. | Hacienda Heights, CA

How do you make a hot dog stand?

Take away its chair.

Aarnav K. | Nashville, TN

Knock Knock.

Who's there?

Figs.

Figs who?

Figs the door bell, it's broken!

Alaina H. | East Haven, CT

What do farmers plant in their sofas?

Couch potatoes.

MacKinley M. | Shelby Township, MI

Why did the corn dislike the farmer?

He was always pulling their ears.

Carl D. | Kansas City, MO

Why did the chicken want to be in the band?

Because he wanted to play the drumsticks.

Destiny P. | Cypress, CA

Why was the cookie sad?

Because his mom was wafer so long.

Conner S. | Lenoir City, TN

Why couldn't the monkey catch the banana?

The banana split.

MacKinley M. | Shelby Township, MI

What did one egg say to the other egg?

"You crack me up!"

Benjamin P. | Wausau, WI

What is an astronaut's favorite sandwich filling?

Launch meat!

Sydney F. | Agawam, MA

What does Darth Vader order when he goes into a bakery?

Only one cannoli.

Elizabeth F. | Wharton, NJ

What do you call an animal that's half parrot and half Godzilla?

Give up? Me too. But if it asked for a cracker he'd get it!

Jaylin J. | Charlotte, NC

Knock Knock.

Who's there?

Lettuce.

Lettuce who?

Lettuce in, it's freezing out here!

Samson G. | Saint Louis, MO

What did sushi A say to sushi B?

"Wassap B!"

Ayla L. | San Diego, CA

Knock Knock.

Who's there?

Nacho.

Nacho who?

I'm nacho who myself.

James O. | Wauwatosa, WI

What did the police do with the hamburger?

They grilled him.

MacKinley M. | Shelby Township, MI

What do you call a berry patch on a really windy day?

Blew berries.

Isaiah R. | Otsego, MN

Where does the spaghetti go to dance?

To the meat ball.

Destiny P. | Cypress, CA

Why did the bird cross the kitchen?

(Say quickly) To eat! To eat! (tweet tweet)

Parker S. | Farmington, MN

Do you think that chicken soup is good for you?

Not if you are a chicken!

Alaena M. | Bloomfield Twp, MI

What kind of bike does a balloon ride?

A popsicle.

Hailey C. | Red Oak, TX

What kind of sauce is really scared?

Alfredo sauce!

Maci B. | Denton, MD

UnitedHealthcare Children's Foundation

Two melons are on a date.

Melon 1: Honey, do you love me?

Melon 2: Cantalope, we'll always be together.

Torben N. | Plymouth, MN

Why did the cookie go to the doctor?

Because he felt crumby!

Jase G. | Savannah, TX

What does the tomato say to the other tomato in a race?

"Catch up!"

Colin M. | Vallejo, CA

What do you call a witch that lives in the desert?

A sand-wich!

Carson E. | Plymouth, MN

What's a dog's favorite pizza topping?

Pupperoni.

Zachary B. | Foothill Ranch, CA

Why did the potato go to France?

Because it wanted to be a French fry!

Sebastian T. | Phoenix, AZ

What's the jam that nobody likes?

A traffic jam.

Faith N. | Tampa, FL

What did the cookie say to the chocolate?

"I need some of your chips!"

Kasey C. | Red Oak, TX

Why is the mushroom always happy?

Because he is a fun guy (fungi).

Aashka B. | Tampa, FL

Knock Knock.

Who's there?

Ice.

Ice who?

Ice scream for ice cream!

Yahteira L. | Winston Salem, NC

What did the berry say to the other berry?

"You're looking berry good today."

Zabella G. | Devine, TX

How do you make gold soup?

You put 24 carrots in it!

Akshara G. | Plymouth, MN

What do you get when you cross the sun with a puppy?

A hot dog!

Lauren S. | Rumford, RI

What did the grape say when it got stepped on?

Not a word. It just let out a little wine.

Ayla L. | San Diego, CA

What do you get when you cross a basketball team with cinnamon crullers?

Dunkin' Donuts.

MacKinley M. | Shelby Township, MI

When do you go on red and stop on green?

When you're eating a watermelon!

Amrita G. | Plymouth, MN

Why can't you tell secrets in a garden?

Because the potatoes have eyes, the corn has ears, and the beans stalk.

James O. | Wauwatosa, WI

**What do you get when you put
a cow on a trampoline?**

A milkshake.

Hunter M. | Granby, CT

What do whales like to eat on their toast?

"Jelly" fish!

Jackson C. | Derry, NH

**A little girl walks up to her mom's bed right
before she was going to sleep and puts a few
candies under the pillow.**

Her mom asks "Why did you do that?"

**The little girl says "I want you to have
sweet dreams."**

Amber J. | Hacienda Heights, CA

Why did the orange go to the doctor?

Because he wasn't peeling well.

Brooklyn L. | Duluth, MN

What is the best thing to put in a birthday cake?

Your teeth!

Owen B. | Huntingdon, PA

If you know any vegetable jokes, please LETTUCE know.

Vineet K. | Eden Prairie, MN

How do you know carrots are good for your eyes?

You never see a rabbit wearing glasses.

Ian S. | Denham Springs, LA

What kind of pet does a taco have?

A beanie dog!

Isabella V. | Great Falls, MT

What did the bread do on vacation?

It loafed around.

Amayah J. | Palm Bay, FL

What kind of eggs do evil chickens lay?

Deviled eggs.

Elliana D. | Duluth, MN

What did the Coke say to the ice cream?

"Let's float!"

Ella Jean A. | Germantown, TN

What is Pop's favorite candy?

Lollipop.

Braidy K. | Mondovi, WI

Why did the students eat their homework?

Because the teacher said it was a piece of cake!

Ethan L. | Phoenix, AZ

What do you call a toothless bear?

A Gummy Bear.

Maddison W. | Marysville, WA

What did the sheep eat for lunch?

A baaaa-logna sandwich.

Hazel S. I Lehi, UT

How did the jury find the hamburger?

Grill-ty as charred.

Juldyz W. I Buffalo, MN

What do you call a shoe that is made from a banana?

A slipper.

Zayda L. I Scottsdale, AZ

What is a Grammy's favorite snack?

A graham cracker.

Kaylee G. I Hooksett, NH

What did the tongue say to the naughty ice cream cone?

"I'm gonna give you a lickin."

Paige R. I Hillsborough, NJ

What do you get when a cow and a smurf collide?

Blue cheese.

Mia S. | Castle Rock, CO

What is a hyena's favorite candy?

Laffy Taffy.

Nathan G. | Tampa, FL

Why do potatoes make good detectives?

They always keep their eyes peeled!

Akshara G. | Plymouth, MN

My sister bet me I couldn't build a car out of spaghetti.

You should've seen the look on her face when I drove pasta!

Corey W. | Cookeville, TN

What did the vinaigrette say to the lettuce?

"Shut the door, I'm dressing!"

Caitlyn I. | Salem, NH

Knock Knock.

Who's there?

Doughnut.

Doughnut who?

Doughnut ask, it's a secret!

Nate F. | Weston, FL

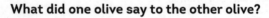

What did one olive say to the other olive?

"Olive you."

Maddox D. | Duluth, MN

What beans do not grow in the ground?

Jelly beans.

Zabella G. | Devine, TX

What drink do you carry in an ambulance?

A Kool-AID.

Sanjeev B. | Ellicott City, MD

How does Lady Gaga like her steak?

Raw, raw, raw, raw, raw!

Aiden B. | San Benito, TX

Why do French people eat snails?

Because they don't like fast food!

Calvin B. | Columbia, SC

Why did the man get fired from the orange juice factory?

Because he couldn't concentrate!

Alice C. | New Prague, MN

Knock Knock.

Who's there?

Pizza.

Pizza who?

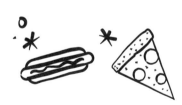

Pizza really great guy!

Derek R. | Old Bridge, NJ

What kind of fish goes best with peanut butter?

Jelly fish.

Benjamin P. | Bloomington, MN

What do you get when you plant tears?

BLUEberries!

Garrett S. | Godfrey, IL

Why did the strawberry call the police?

Because it was in a jam.

Sophie B. | Thomasville, NC

What do ducks have for snack?

Milk and quackers!

Anonymous

What did the police officer say to the popsicle?

"Freeze!"

Jackson S. | Lilburn, GA

UnitedHealthcare Children's Foundation

What kind of nut doesn't have a shell?

A doughnut!

CJ M. | Reeds Spring, MO

What do eggs like to do?

KaraYOKE.

Alexa H. | Clear Lake, IA

What are mountains' favorite type of candy?

Snow Caps.

Megan V. | Castleton, NY

Why did the tofu cross the road?

To prove he wasn't chicken.

Zurrie L. | Scottsdale, AZ

Did you hear about the guy who got hit in the head with a can of soda?

He was lucky it was a soft drink.

Ethan J. | Las Vegas, NV

What kind of fish grow on trees?

Fish sticks!

Lauren W. | Onalaska, WI

What does an annoying pepper do?

Gets JALAPENO face!

Hadley N. | Bristol, TN

What do you call a pig that knows karate?

A pork chop.

Sophie B. | Thomasville, NC

How do you catch a monkey?

Climb up a tree and act like a banana.

Hunter N. | Bloomington, MN

What is the most musical part of a chicken?

The drumstick!

Ayden R. | Chico, CA

UnitedHealthcare Children's Foundation

Son: Mom, isn't all ketchup made from tomatoes?

Mom: Yes.

Son: Why do they all say "tomato ketchup" on the bottle?

Mom: Sometimes I think you might already be smarter than me.

Oliver E. | Willard, MO

What do you call a piece of cheese that likes to shoot hoops?

Swiss-hh!

Zakarya F. | Indianapolis, IN

What did the bacon say to the tomato?

"Lettuce get together!"

Theo N. | East Hampton, CT

How do pilots like their hot dogs?

Plane.

Darien M. | Rome, NY

Why did the elephant sit on the marshmallow?

Because he didn't want to fall in the cocoa.

Nathan K. | Eagan, MN

What do you call pigs playing tug of war?

Pulled pork!

Elizabeth L. | Durham, CT

How many doughnuts can fit in an empty bag?

One, because then it is not empty.

Sathvik K. | Carlsbad, CA

Two muffins are cooking in the oven.

The first muffin says, "Wow! It's hot in here!"

The second muffin says, "Holy cow, a talking muffin!"

Gary B. | Allen, TX

Why was the salad embarrassed?

Because it had no dressing.

James O. | Wauwatosa, WI

Knock Knock.

Who's there?

Taco.

Taco who?

Tac-o bout awesome!

Caitlyn I. I Salem, NH

Why did the boy jump up and down before he drank his juice?

The carton said to "shake well before drinking."

Haiden C. I West Valley City, UT

Knock Knock.

Who's there?

Handsome.

Handsome who?

Handsome of that popcorn over here!

Lucy C. I Glendale, AZ

What is red, white, blue, and yellow?

The Star-Spangled Banana.

Miranda S. | Green Bay, WI

What does the cheese say when playing basketball?

"Swiss!"

Zakarya F. | Indianapolis, IN

What do you call a shaking cow?

Beef jerky!

Isabella V. | Great Falls, MT

Knock Knock.

Who's there?

Eye (pointing to eye).

Eye who?

I (pointing to self) need some ice cream quick!

Novkov N. | Saint Paul, MN

What does a mermaid eat?

A sand-wich.

Kiersten T. | Madison, MS

What time is it, when it's time to go to the dentist?

Tooth hurty!

Kristin M. | Las Vegas, NV

What are a computer programmer's favorite snacks?

Cookies and cache-ws.

Nandini R. | North Barrington, IL

What do you call cheese that's not yours?

Nacho cheese!

Ava V. | Yorktown Heights, NY

What do cats eat for breakfast?

Mice Krispies!

Alaena M. | Bloomfield Twp, MI

What is the name of a soda that gives out presents on Christmas?

Fanta.

Tim L. | Champlin, MN

What is a dog's favorite breakfast?

Woof-les.

Nico T. | Las Vegas, NV

What did the employees at a Minnesota office do to cut back on sugar consumption?

They started drinking Minne-sotas (mini sodas).

Conor K. | Lombard, IL

Why was the meat afraid to jump in the soup?

Because it was chicken!

Sadie J. | Phoenix, AZ

What did the shark say after he ate a clown fish?

"This fish tastes funny!"

Shavn M. | Atlanta, GA

UnitedHealthcare Children's Foundation

What is a burger's favorite color?

Burgundy.

Adrienne B. | Las Vegas, NV

Want to hear a pizza joke?

Never mind, it's too cheesy.

Jordan O. | Mesa, AZ

What is a french fries' favorite day?

FRY-day.

Noah H. | Clermont, FL

What is a French cat's favorite dessert?

Chocolate mousse!

Tony W. | Buffalo, MN

Where do butchers dance?

At the meat ball.

MacKinley M. | Shelby Township, MI

What is a dog's favorite snack?

Ruff-les.

Nico T. | Las Vegas, NV

What do you call a sheep that takes karate lessons?

Lamb chop!

Isabela N. | Hudson, FL

Why did the journalist go to the ice cream parlor?

She wanted to get the scoop.

MacKinley M. | Shelby Township, MI

Why don't oysters share their pearls?

Because they're shellfish.

Evan D. | Shakopee, MN

How can you tell when a train is eating?

When it chew-chews!

Connor J. | San Antonio, TX

Why did the boy put candy under his pillow?

Because he wanted sweet dreams.

Juldyz W. | Buffalo, MN

Knock Knock.

Who's there?

Ada.

Ada who?

Ada lot of sweets and now I feel sick!

Jack B. | Boise, ID

How are bananas so flexible?

They can do splits.

Christian F. | La Palma, CA

What do you call a dog in the hot summer?

A hot dog!

Vanessa R. | Las Vegas, NV

Never tell me a joke when I am eating. It is way too hard to digest them both.

Darasimi L. | Plainfield, NJ

How do you fix a broken pizza?

With tomato paste.

Isabel A. | Naperville, IL

Why did the root beer sink in the pool?

Because he lost his float.

James O. | Wauwatosa, WI

What type of candy is never on time?

ChocoLATE.

Amrita G. | Plymouth, MN

What did O'Henry say when a zombie's hands fell off?

"Butterfingers!"

Olivia S. | East Haven, CT

UnitedHealthcare Children's Foundation

What is a pirate's favorite fast food place?

ARRRRRby's.

Ainzleigh Q. | West Valley City, UT

What did the green grape say to the purple grape?

"BREATHE! BREATHE!"

Brianna T. | West Winfield, NY

Can you name two burgers that are royalty?

Sirloin and Burger King.

Juldyz W. | Buffalo, MN

What is a chocolate bar made of?

A lot of chalk.

Adelaide G. | Grand Junction, CO

A box of french fries says to a bottle of ketchup and mustard, "I bet you can't guess what my favorite day is?"

"FRI-day!"

Jaylen A. | Glen Burnie, MD

My dad lost his job at the M&M factory!

How did that happen?

He threw away all the "W's"!

Hailey A. | Cape Girardeau, MO

What does a 6-foot-tall butcher weigh?

Meat!

Dylan P. | Scotia, NY

What has ears, but can't hear a thing?

A cornfield.

Lukas V. | Cincinnati, OH

How can you keep from getting a sharp pain in your eye when you drink chocolate milk?

Take the spoon out of your glass!

Tony W. | Buffalo, MN

What did the farmer say to the DJ?

"Turnip the music and lettuce dance."

Luca E. | Phoenix, AZ

UnitedHealthcare Children's Foundation

Where do pretzels come from?

Pretzelvania!

Joshua Q. | Hendersonville, TN

What is a cat's favorite condiment?

MEOW-onnaise.

Eric M. | Albuquerque, NM

A boy asks his father, "Dad, are bugs good to eat?"

"That's disgusting don't talk about things like that over dinner," the dad replies.

After dinner the father asks, "Now, son, what did you want to ask me?"

"Oh, nothing," the boy says. "There was a bug in your soup, but now it's gone."

Jackson T. | Naugatuck, CT

Why wouldn't you want to be stranded on a desserted island?

Because it's made of chocolate and ice cream isn't it?

Anonymous

What did the ketchup say to the hot dog?

"Sup dog? Let's ketch-up!"

Noah H. | Clermont, FL

Why were the socks in the fruit bowl?

Because they were a pear.

Emma F. | Chaska, MN

How do fish become fish sticks?

They fall from a fish tree.

Richard D. | Seattle, WA

What did one jar of jam say to the other jar of jam in a crate?

"I feel jammed."

Anoushka K. | Richmond Hill, GA

Why did the banana go to the doctor?

It wasn't peeling well.

Katie B. | Thomasville, NC

UnitedHealthcare Children's Foundation

What do you get if a cow is in an earthquake?

A milk shake.

Gabby G. | Tampa, FL

What do you call an angry carrot?

A steamed veggie.

Jaden M. | Beaumont, TX

Why was the blueberry so sad?

Because he was blue!

Aryan P. | Shakopee, MN

What is a cow's favorite vegetable?

A moo-shroom.

Addyson W. | Weston, WI

What makes cheese family friendly?

It's G-rated.

Dominic E. | Los Molinos, CA

What fruit is best to drink with?

A STRAWberry!

Kelsey L. | Ocean Isle Beach, NC

Why do they call it Russian dressing?

Because it's "Russian" out of the bottle.

Isabel C. | Brookhaven, PA

What is a computer's favorite snack?

A computer chip!

Darius G. | Maple Grove, MN

How do kitty cats keep their milk cold?

With mice cubes!

Claire G. | Des Moines, IA

What is one thing an ice cream monster is afraid of?

A spoon!

Sam L. | Lakewood, WA

UnitedHealthcare
Children's Foundation

What do you call a swimming melon?

A watermelon.

Leen A. | Orange, CA

Knock Knock.

Who's there?

Gorilla.

Gorilla who?

Gorilla me a hamburger... I'm hungry!

Haiden C. | West Valley City, UT

Hurry Doctor, I need glasses!

"Yes you do sir, this is a restaurant!"

Ryan E. | Otsego, MN

Knock Knock.

Who's there?

Orange!

Orange who?

Orange you glad I didn't say banana?

Callaigh U. | Romulus, MI

What's worse than finding a worm in your apple?

Finding only half a worm in your apple.

Tony W. | Buffalo, MN

Why did the bear stop eating?

Because he was stuffed.

Destiny P. | Cypress, CA

What do you get when a cold dog sits on a bunny?

A chili dog on a bun.

Hayden S. | Chippewa Falls, WI

What kind of pie do ghosts like?

Boo berry!

Jordyn C. | Manvel, TX

What is a monster's favorite snack?

Sugar Babies!

Gianna S. | East Haven, CT

UnitedHealthcare
Children's Foundation

Why can't a doughnut do yoga?

Because they can never "find their center".

Salma A. | Weston, FL

What is Bruce Lee's favorite drink?

Wat-aaaaaaaa.

Bailey H. | Raleigh, NC

How do you make a milkshake?

Give it a good scare!

Lily H. | Fishers, IN

What is black, white, and red all over?

A penguin eating strawberries. He was very messy!

Mia R. | Duluth, MN

Where do baby cows like to eat their veggies?

In the Calf-ateria!

Sydney S. | Long Valley, NJ

Knock Knock.

Who's there?

Doughnut.

Doughnut who?

Knock Knock.

Who's there?

Doughnut.

Doughnut who?

Doughnut ask me again.

James O. | Wauwatosa, WI

What did the baby corn say to the mama corn?

"Where's POP-corn?"

Maya B. | Bristow, VA

What do you call Chewbacca when he has chocolate stuck in his hair?

A chocolate chip Wookiee.

Juldyz W. | Buffalo, MN

UnitedHealthcare Children's Foundation

Why don't zombies eat ice cream?

It gives them BRAAAAIIIINNN freeze.

Laura K. | Forest Lake, MN

Did you hear about the the Italian chef?

He pasta way.

Joel G. | Gulf Breeze, FL

Why did the doughnut go to the dentist?

Because it needed a chocolate filling.

Sophie H. | Fishers, IN

What do you call a sad strawberry?

A blue berry.

Amanda A. | Las Vegas, NV

Why did the boy plant an egg in the garden?

He wanted an eggplant.

Vincent B. | Beallsville, MD

Why was the spaghetti sent to bed?

Because it was pasta's bedtime.

Mason P. | Flourtown, PA

What is the favorite sport of hamburgers and hot dogs?

Ketchup baseball.

Randall C. | Shakopee, MN

What do they serve at birthday parties in heaven?

Angel food cake.

Kelsey T. | Plant City, FL

Knock Knock.

Who's there?

Olive.

Olive who?

Awe - I love you too!

Molly Z. | Newington, CT

UnitedHealthcare Children's Foundation

Knock Knock.

Who's there?

Orange.

Orange who?

Orange you gonna give me a kiss?

Gabriela C. | St. Petersburg, FL

Can you tell what a cantaloupe is?

It is a cross between a camel and an antelope.

Philip H. | Hillsdale, WY

Why did you throw the butter out the window?

Because I wanted to see the BUTTER-FLY!

Vineet K. | Eden Prairie, MN

Why was the tomato blushing?

Because it saw the salad dressing.

Allie S. | Macungie, PA

What do you call a dancing pig?

Shakin' bacon.

Tatum R. | New Orleans, LA

What is a Greek god's favorite cheese?

Gorgon-zola.

Yair W. | Rockaway Park, NY

Why was the apple tree so sad?

Because it was always picked on!

Miranda Z. | Three Bridges, NJ

How do you know it's cold outside?

When you milk a brown cow you get chocolate ice cream!

Jacob S. | Wausau, WI

What do you call a fake noodle?

An impasta!

Alice C. | New Prague, MN

Why don't eggs make good quarterbacks?

When their defense cracks, they're too quick to scramble.

MacKinley M. | Shelby Township, MI

What type of fruit likes battleships?

Navel oranges!

August S. | Minnetonka, MN

What is a shark's favorite pizza topping?

People-roni.

Branda'nae S. | Columbus, OH

Knock Knock.

Who's there?

Justin.

Justin who?

Justin time for dinner!

CJ M. | Reeds Spring, MO

Why did the lady take the doughnut back to the store?

Because there was a hole in it.

Xavier S. I Orlando, FL

What is Thomas the Train's favorite treat to eat?

A cheese PUFF!

Jackson J. I Banner Elk, NC

Knock Knock.

Who's there?

Ketchup.

Ketchup who?

Ketchup or you'll be late for school.

Cody L. I Tolland, CT

What do you get when you put eyes on a cucumber?

A sea cucumber.

Henrik F. I Chaska, MN

UnitedHealthcare Children's Foundation

What did the clock do after dinner?

He had seconds!

What did he do after seconds?

He washed his hands!

Madison L. | Carlsbad, CA

Why do bees have sticky hair?

Because they use honeycombs!

Abigail B. | Cairo, NY

What did the doughnut say to the doughnut hole?

"You complete me!"

Leo F. | Weston, FL

What is a frog's favorite meal from McDonald's?

Cheeseburger and flies!

Macy D. | Shakopee, MN

What did the eggplant say to the other eggplant?

Nothing! Eggplants can't talk!

Leilani N. | Orlando, FL

Why did the orange stop in the middle the road?

He ran out of juice.

Miranda S. | Green Bay, WI

What did Mr. and Mrs. Hamburger name their daughter?

Patty.

Autumn H. | Shakopee, MN

Knock Knock.

Who's there?

Pop.

Pop who?

Popsicle.

Ella Jean A. | Germantown, TN

Why was the man's jelly gun stuck?

Because it was jammed!

Grey M. | Winchester, VA

What kind of keys do kids like to eat?

Cookies.

Darius G. | Maple Grove, MN

What do you give a sick lemon?

Lemon-aid.

Landon L. | Saint Johns, FL

What kind of bagel can fly?

A plain bagel.

Zurrie L. | Scottsdale, AZ

What are single fruits jealous of?

The pears (pairs).

Anshul N. | Springfield, IL

Knock Knock.

Who's there?

Ice cream!

Ice cream who?

Ice cream if you throw me in the cold, cold water!

Sophie H. | Fishers, IN

What kind of cheese is made backwards?

Edam.

Miles A. | Naperville, IL

What kind of doughnuts can fly?

A plane one!

Zaid A. | Weston, FL

What do you do if you see a blue banana?

Try to cheer it up.

Anonymous

What is a candy's favorite thing to do?

Be sweet!

Braidy K. | Mondovi, WI

Why was the pickle laughing so much?

Because he was pickle-ish.

Asha P. | N. Las Vegas, NV

What did one hot dog say to the other hot dog?

"What's cooking Frank."

Gavin G. | Pembroke, NH

Which letter is the coolest?

Ice T.

Alyssa S. | Denham Springs, LA

What do you get if you cross a sweet potato with a jazz musician?

A yam session!

Dezi W. | Buffalo, MN

What do you call a Dauschund with a fever?

A hot dog.

Emily B. | Louisville, KY

How many stars are in the Milky Way?

None, just sugar.

Julian F. | Washington, DC

What happens when you run through a sprinkler?

You get covered in sprinkles.

Cody L. | Tolland, CT

What kind of key unlocks a banana?

A monkey!

Sullivan F. | Maumee, OH

What does a duck say to the waiter at the end of his meal?

"Just put it on my bill!"

Harry W. | Edmond, OK

What do you call a cow with a twitch?

Beef jerky!

Brianna T. | West Winfield, NY

Knock Knock.

Who's there?

Nunya.

Nunya who?

Nunya business.

Zoey R. | Brooklyn Park, MN

Where do vegetables go to college?

Kale University!

Alex K. | Jenkintown, PA

What is a nut's favorite book?

The Almondnac.

Blaine P. | Alexandria, VA

What did the orange say to the banana when they were looking for the apple?

"Keep your eyes peeled."

Kelsey C. | Phoenix, AZ

What does the mummy do when he spits out his gum?

He puts it in his wrapper!

Colin M. | Vallejo, CA

What did the candy bride call her groom on their wedding day?

SweeTARTS.

Sean H. | Menomonee Falls, WI

What did the half a stick of butter say to its other half?

"You're my butter half."

Jordan R. | Plano, TX

What do you call a crate full of ducks?

A box of quackers!

Luke B. | Smyrna, TN

What do spiders eat in Paris?

French flies!

Andy M. | Damascus, OR

What tastes better than it smells?

A tongue.

Ethan J. | Las Vegas, NV

What candy do you eat on the playground?

Recess Pieces.

Rachel Q. | Apple Valley, MN

What school does ice cream go to?

Sundae school.

Anna A. | Surprise, AZ

What is a rock's favorite candy?

Pop Rocks.

Braidy K. | Mondovi, WI

Why didn't the egg get the joke?

Because it was a little scrambled.

Anonymous

What kind of apple isn't really an apple?

A pineapple.

Jerred L. | Houston, TX

Why were the Fruit Loops afraid of the milk?

Because they heard it was a cereal killer.

Tate S. | Sylva, NC

What does a polar bear eat for lunch?

Iceberg-ers!

Andy M. | Damascus, OR

UnitedHealthcare Children's Foundation

How do you make a nut laugh?

Crack it up!

Autumn H. | Shakopee, MN

What do you get when you give an elephant potatoes?

Smashed potatoes.

Sophia C. | Cypress, CA

Knock Knock.

Who's there?

Dishes.

Dishes who?

Dishes a bad joke.

Evan R. | Las Vegas, NV

What do you call a nosey pepper?

Jalapeno business.

Hanna S. | Round Rock, TX

How are baseball and cake alike?

They both need batters!

Alice C. | New Prague, MN

Why is 6 afraid of 7?

Because seven eight (ate) nine.

Colt D. | Sacramento, CA

What is orange and sounds like a parrot?

A carrot.

Mason C. | Green Bay, WI

What didn't the giant eat for dinner?

Breakfast and lunch!

JP R. | Tucson, AZ

What has a hole in it and everyone buys it instead of throwing it away?

A doughnut.

Kasey C. | Red Oak, TX

UnitedHealthcare Children's Foundation

If the vegetables had a race who would win?

The lettuce, by a head.

Gigi G. | Lansdale, PA

What do you call a popsicle outside?

Melted.

Samuel Z. | Menifee, CA

"Waiter, will my pizza be long?"

"No sir, it will be round."

Tony W. | Buffalo, MN

If "can't" is short for "cannot", what is "don't" short for?

Doughnut!

Kareem A. | Weston, FL

Why did the candies get an "A" on the test?

Because they were Smarties.

Anna A. | Surprise, AZ

What do you get when you cross a centipede with a chicken?

Enough wings for everyone!

Ella L. | Falls Church, VA

What wobbles in the sky?

A jelly-copter!

Hazley W. | Crystal, MN

Knock Knock.

Who's there?

Peas.

Peas who?

Peas pass the salt.

Jordan R. | Plano, TX

What did the big tomato say to the little tomato?

"Come on, ketchup!"

Josie H. | Kent, UK

What do you call pancakes, bacon, and eggs on a scale?

A balanced breakfast.

Anna A. | Surprise, AZ

How can you tell that clocks are always hungry?

They have seconds!

Sawyer G. | Saint Louis, MO

How do you win over a chocolate lover?

By keeping some Twix up your sleeves!

Rebecca A. | Chicago, IL

Knock Knock.

Who's there?

Doughnut.

Doughnut who?

We doughnut have classes during summer.

Gabe B. | Slidell, LA

What is a sea mammal's favorite drink?

A mana-tea!

Milo H. | St. Petersburg, FL

How do monsters like their eggs?

Terri-fried!

Megan P. | Islip, NY

Why did the farmer pick all the strawberries?

Because it was the ripe thing to do!

Charlie K. | Plymouth, MN

Why do watermelons have fancy weddings?

Because they cantaloupe.

Brayden R. | Dublin, OH

How do you pronounce a cooked letter "E"?

Cookie.

Jordin H. | Compton, CA

Knock Knock.

Who's there?

Bacon.

Bacon who?

I'm bacon treats for you.

Gabe B. | Slidell, LA

What is a cow's favorite summer food?

Smooooooothie.

Anton K. | Minnetonka, MN

Why was the strawberry worried?

Because his parents got jammed.

Evan J. | Schofield, WI

Knock Knock.

Who's there?

Barba.

Barba who?

Barbaque!

David W. | Forest Hills, NY

A neutron walks into a ice cream parlor, orders an ice cream and asks, "How much for ice cream?"

The salesperson replies, "For you, no charge!"

Joseph B. | Gaithersburg, MD

What kind of cake do you eat in the bathtub?

A sponge cake.

Paige R. | Hillsborough, NJ

How much is one sundae plus one sundae?

None because I ate them all!

Scotty N. | Sylvania, OH

What kind of cup can hold no water?

A cupcake!

Macy D. | Shakopee, MN

Mom told me it's not safe to chase after cars, so I chase the ice cream truck instead.

Isaac D. | Buckingham, IA

YOU CAN BECOME ONE OF THE AUTHORS!

Jot down your own favorite jokes here!

_____

_____

_____

_____

_____

_____

_____

_____

_____

_____

_____

_____

_____

_____

_____

_____

_____

_____

_____

_____

_____

_____

_____

_____

_____

_____

_____

_____

_____

_____

_____

_____

_____

_____

_____

_____

_____

_____

_____

_____

_____

_____

_____

_____

_____

_____

_____

_____

_____

_____

_____

_____

_____

_____

_____

_____

_____

_____

_____

_____

_____

_____

_____

Discover fun
activities and downloads,
when you visit
Oliver & Hope's©
Clubhouse at
vhccf.org/OliverandHope.

FIND OLIVER & HOPE® BOOKS, GIFTS AND MORE AT

vhccf.org/shop

UnitedHealthcare Children's Foundation